WILD RIDES

Superbikes

An Hachette UK Company
www.hachette.co.uk

First published in Great Britain in 2012 by
TickTock, a division of Octopus Publishing Group Ltd
Endeavour House
189 Shaftesbury Avenue
London
WC2H 8JY
www.octopusbooks.co.uk

ISBN 978 1 84898 636 7

A CIP catalogue record for this book is available from the British Library

Printed and bound in China

10 9 8 7 6 5 4 3 2 1

Picture credits:
All images Car Photo Library—www.carphoto.co.uk.

Every effort has been made to trace the copyright holders, and we apologise in advance for any unintentional omissions. We would be pleased to insert the appropriate acknowledgments in any subsequent edition of this publication.

Contents

Aprilia RSV Mille R 4

Benelli Tornado 6

Buell XB9R Firebolt 8

Honda CBR1100XX Blackbird 10

Kawasaki Ninja ZX-12R 12

Mondial Piega 14

Harley V-Rod 16

Cagiva V-Raptor 1000 18

Ducati 999R 20

MV Agusta F4 SPR Senna 22

Suzuki GSX 1300R Hayabusa 24

Triumph Daytona 955i 26

Yamaha YZF R1 28

Glossary 30

Index 32

The Italian company Aprilia first became known as a maker of bicycles. In 1968, it began producing motorcycles and mopeds. In 2002, Aprilia launched the Mille R. This beautiful machine was big, fast and very comfortable. The 'R' stands for racing, since this bike was the fastest machine Aprilia ever made.

DID YOU KNOW?

'Mille' means 'one thousand' in Italian. The RVS was called Mille because the engine was almost 1,000 cc.

Until 2001, all Mille Rs were single-seat bikes. In 2002, Aprilia made a two-seater version.

One of the most eye-catching features of the Aprilia was its triple headlight.

The Mille had special radial brakes at the front. These were extra strong, so the bike could stop very quickly.

STATS & FACTS

LAUNCHED: 2002

ORIGIN: ITALY

ENGINE: 997.6 CC

CYLINDERS: 2

MAXIMUM POWER: 128 BHP AT 9,500 RPM

MAXIMUM TORQUE: 101 NM AT 7,400 RPM

GEARS: 6

DRY WEIGHT: 168 KG

MAXIMUM SPEED: 270.4 KM/H (168 MPH)

FUEL TANK CAPACITY: 18 LITRES

COLOURS: APRILIA BLACK OR FLASHY YELLOW

COST: £9,999

Benelli Tornado

In 1911, Italian widow Teresa Benelli founded the Benelli Mechanical Workshop to provide jobs for her six sons. The company, which started by making spare parts for cars and motorcycles, produced its first motorcycle in 1921. In 2002, Benelli launched the Tornado, a 260.7 km/h (162 mph) superbike. Only 150 bikes were produced, but other models followed: the Tornado Tre 1130 was introduced in 2006. It had a maximum power of 161 bhp at 10,500 rpm.

The engine was also part of the frame. This made the bike stronger.

DID YOU KNOW?

Built in Italy, this bike was designed by Adrian Morton, an Englishman. The suspension was made in Sweden.

The Tornado's radiator was under the seat. Two big fans sucked in air to cool the radiator.

A racing version of the Tornado competed at the World Superbike Series. It was designed by Riccardo Rosa, who worked for Ferrari.

STATS & FACTS

LAUNCHED: 2002

ORIGIN: ITALY

ENGINE: 898 CC

CYLINDERS: 3

MAXIMUM POWER: 147 BHP AT 11,500 RPM

MAXIMUM TORQUE: 100 NM AT 8,500 RPM

GEARS: 6

DRY WEIGHT: 185 KG

MAXIMUM SPEED: 260.7 KM/H (162 MPH)

FUEL TANK CAPACITY: 18 LITRES

COLOURS: GREEN/SILVER

COST: £22,000

Buell XB9R Firebolt

Made between 2001 and 2005, the Firebolt was the brainchild of Erik Buell. A former Harley-Davidson engineer, he wanted to put a Harley engine in a lighter bike to make a really fast machine. Buell worked with Harley-Davidson to create 136,923 bikes before stopping production in 2009. He now works on his own to produce the racing Buell 1125R and the street 1190RS.

The Firebolt had unusual features. The exhaust pipe was underneath the Firebolt. It also had a hollow frame, which stored gasoline.

DID YOU KNOW?

Weighing just 175 kg, the Firebolt was one of the lightest superbikes in the world.

The Firebolt had perimeter brakes at the front. The brake disc was much bigger than normal, which allowed the motorcycle to stop quickly.

The Firebolt had a belt instead of a chain to make the back wheel turn.

STATS & FACTS

LAUNCHED: 2002

ORIGIN: US

ENGINE: 984 CC

CYLINDERS: 2

MAXIMUM POWER: 92 BHP AT 7,200 RPM

MAXIMUM TORQUE: 92 NM AT 5,500 RPM

GEARS: 5

DRY WEIGHT: 175 KG

MAXIMUM SPEED: 209 KM/H (130 MPH)

FUEL TANK CAPACITY: 14 LITRES

COLOURS: WHITE, BATTLE BLUE

COST: £7,345

Honda CBR1100XX Blackbird

The Japanese company Honda wanted to design the fastest motorcycle ever. In 1996, it created the Blackbird, named after the Lockheed SR-71 aircraft, another record holder. With a few tweaks, the Blackbird could rocket to an incredible 320 km/h (200 mph). In 1999, Suzuki stole Honda's thunder with the Hayabusa (see pp.24-25).

DID YOU KNOW?

In 2001, a rider on a turbo-charged Blackbird did a wheelie at an amazing 320 km/h (200 mph)!

The Blackbird had linked brakes. When the rider pulled the front brake lever the back brake worked, too. The back brake pedal also controlled the front brake pedal.

The Honda CBR900RR Fireblade was smaller, lighter, and faster than the Blackbird. It could go from 0 to 160 km/h (100 mph) in 6 seconds.

STATS & FACTS

LAUNCHED: 1996

ORIGIN: JAPAN

ENGINE: 1,137 CC

CYLINDERS: 4

MAXIMUM POWER: 164 BHP AT 9,200 RPM

MAXIMUM TORQUE: 116 NM AT 7,300 RPM

GEARS: 6

DRY WEIGHT: 223 KG

MAXIMUM SPEED: 320 KM/H (200 MPH)

FUEL TANK CAPACITY: 24 LITRES

COLOURS: BLACK, BLUE, RED

COST: £10,500

Thanks to its streamlined shape and huge engine, this bike could race from 0 to 209 km/h (130 mph) in 11 seconds.

Kawasaki Ninja ZX-12R

The Japanese company Kawasaki has always made very fast motorcycles. Produced from 2000 to 2006, the ZX-12R was one of the fastest bikes on the planet, capable of just under 320 km/h (200 mph). The Ninja also had a big fuel tank, so it could travel long distances.

The ZX-12R could go from 113 km/h (70 mph) to a complete stop in under 4 seconds.

DID YOU KNOW?

The ZX-12R had the widest back tyre of any sports bike. It was a huge 20 cm wide!

The scoop under the headlight forced air into the engine, which dragged extra fuel in. This gave the ZX-12R even more power.

In 2012, the 'king of all sports bikes' was launched. With a 1,441 cc engine, the Ninja ZX-14 is the most powerful production bike ever made.

STATS & FACTS

LAUNCHED: 2000

ORIGIN: JAPAN

ENGINE: 1,199 CC

CYLINDERS: 4

MAXIMUM POWER: 165 BHP AT 9,800 RPM

MAXIMUM TORQUE: 130 NM AT 7,800 RPM

GEARS: 6

DRY WEIGHT: 210 KG

MAXIMUM SPEED: 305.8 KM/H (190 MPH)

FUEL TANK CAPACITY: 20 LITRES

COLOURS: BLACK/GOLD, SILVER, KAWASAKI GREEN

COST: £9,500

Mondial was founded by an Italian named Earls Boselli. His motorcycles won many races in the 1940s and 1950s. The company went out of business in 1967, but in 1997 it began making motorcycles again. The Piega was produced in 120 pieces between 2001 and 2004.

DID YOU KNOW?

In 2006, different owners brought the bike back to the racing circuits. New regulations, however, forced the company to abandon the dream of a superbike.

The Mondial Piega has special radial brakes. They are stronger than ordinary brakes and slow this fiery bike down in record time.

The Piega's fairing is made from carbon fibre. It is only available in silver and blue.

STATS & FACTS

LAUNCHED: 2002

ORIGIN: ITALY

ENGINE: 999 CC

CYLINDERS: 2

MAXIMUM POWER: 140 BHP AT 9,800 RPM

MAXIMUM TORQUE: 100 NM AT 8,800 RPM

GEARS: 6

DRY WEIGHT: 226 KG

MAX SPEED: 259 KM/H (161 MPH)

FUEL TANK CAPACITY: 20 LITRES

COLOURS: SILVER, BLUE

COST: £15,500

The engine in the Mondial is Japanese. It was first used in a Honda motorcycle.

Harley V-Rod

Often associated with the Hell's Angels, the classic Harley-Davidson was made to ride long, straight roads in comfort. In 2002, the company launched a sportier model, the V-Rod. Produced until 2006, it was the fastest bike the company ever made. It was so popular that in 2012 a tenth-anniversary model was produced in limited edition: the V-Rod 10th Anniversary Edition.

The V-Rod had a water-cooled engine. It was designed with the German carmaker Porsche.

DID YOU KNOW?

Even though these were heavy bikes, the stunt rider Evel Knievel did many jumps on a Harley-Davidson.

To celebrate the company's hundred-year anniversary, all bikes made in 2003 featured the Harley-Davidson 100th anniversary tank emblem with chrome bar and shield.

The V-Rod's fuel tank was under the seat. The space this saved left room for air intakes. These forced more fuel into the bike's engine and supplied extra power.

STATS & FACTS

LAUNCHED: 2002

ORIGIN: US

ENGINE: 1,130 CC

CYLINDERS: 2

MAXIMUM POWER: 115 BHP AT 8,000 RPM

MAXIMUM TORQUE: 88 NM AT 6,300 RPM

GEARS: 5

DRY WEIGHT: 270 KG

MAXIMUM SPEED: 217 KM/H (135 MPH)

FUEL TANK CAPACITY: 15.1 LITRES

COLOUR: ANODIZED ALUMINIUM

COST: £13,995

Cagiva V-Raptor 1000

The Cagiva company started with two motorcycles in 1978. A year later, it was building over 40,000 bikes a year. This crazy-looking machine was designed by an Italian named Miguel Galluzzi in 2000. It was a 'naked' sportbike as there was no fairing covering the engine. It combined easy handling and high performance.

DID YOU KNOW?

The name Cagiva is made up of two letters from the founder's last and first names – Ca(stiglioni) Gi(ovanni) – and the first two letters of the company's hometown – Va(rese).

The Cagiva V-Raptor 1000 used an engine made by the Japanese company Suzuki.

This bike had claws! The V-Raptor had a strange set of talons by the passenger footrest.

LAUNCHED: 2000

ORIGIN: ITALY

ENGINE: 996 CC

CYLINDERS: 2

MAXIMUM POWER: 114 BHP AT 8,500 RPM

MAXIMUM TORQUE: 96 NM AT 7,000 RPM

GEARS: 6

DRY WEIGHT: 197 KG

MAXIMUM SPEED: 240 KM/H (149 MPH)

FUEL TANK CAPACITY: 18 LITRES

COLOUR: RED

COST: £7,200

The 'V' in the name described the shape of the two cylinders.

Ducati 999R

Ducati is an Italian motorcycle company that was bought by the German car manufacturer Audi in 2012. The 999 was the fastest and most expensive motorcycle Ducati produced. It was made of carbon fibre and aluminium.

The seat and fuel tank could be moved backward and forward, and the footrests moved up and down. This Ducati was comfortable to ride, whatever your height.

DID YOU KNOW?

The 'R' was based on the same bike that raced in the World Superbike Series.

This is the Ducati 1199 Panigale. The name links the bike to its origins in Borgo Panigale, near Bologna, Italy. The area is called 'Motor Valley'.

Each 999R had a unique silver emblem to prove that it was a limited-edition motorcycle.

STATS & FACTS

LAUNCHED: 2002

ORIGIN: ITALY

ENGINE: 999 CC

CYLINDERS: 2

MAXIMUM POWER: 139 BHP AT 10,000 RPM

MAXIMUM TORQUE: 108 NM AT 8,000 RPM

GEARS: 6

DRY WEIGHT: 193 KG

MAX SPEED: 281.6 KM/H (175 MPH)

FUEL TANK CAPACITY: 15.5 LITRES

COLOURS: RED OR YELLOW

COST: £19,300

MV Agusta F4 SPR Senna

MV Agusta is another Italian company with a racing history. Agusta bikes won 270 Grand Prix races between 1950 and 1975, before the company closed down. In 1999, MV Agusta was brought back to life with the launch of the stunning F4. Many people think the Senna is the most beautiful bike in the world.

DID YOU KNOW?

Only 300 Senna bikes were made in memory of F1 driver Ayrton Senna. They were sold in aid of Brazilian children.

The Senna's twin headlights were arranged on top of each other to make it more aerodynamic.

STATS & FACTS

LAUNCHED: 2002

ORIGIN: ITALY

ENGINE: 749 CC

CYLINDERS: 4

MAXIMUM POWER: 140 BHP AT 12,600 RPM

MAXIMUM TORQUE: 81 NM AT 10,500 RPM

GEARS: 6

DRY WEIGHT: 188 KG

MAXIMUM SPEED: 284.9 KM/H (177 MPH)

FUEL TANK CAPACITY: 20 LITRES

COLOURS: GREY AND RED

COST: £17,350

Suzuki GSX 1300R Hayabusa

The Japanese manufacturer Suzuki was founded in 1952. In 1998, it built a superfast motorcycle called the Hayabusa. In 2000, new safety regulations limited the speed of all new bikes. This model is officially the fastest production bike on Earth, since no other motorcycle can be made to go faster without being altered.

The British Land Speed Record for a motorcycle is held by a turbo-charged Hayabusa. It topped 388 km/h (241 mph)!

DID YOU KNOW?

A Hayabusa is so powerful that it can wear out a back tyre in as little as 1,600 km (1,000 miles).

This is the Hayabusa 2011. Powered by a 1340 cc, 16-valve engine, it is one of the fastest sport bikes currently in production.

The Hayabusa is a bird of prey that eats blackbirds. Suzuki named its new bike Hayabusa because it was faster and more powerful than Honda's Blackbird, its rival.

STATS & FACTS

LAUNCHED: 1998

ORIGIN: JAPAN

ENGINE: 1,298 CC

CYLINDERS: 4

MAXIMUM POWER: 155 BHP AT 9,000 RPM

MAXIMUM TORQUE: 134 NM AT 6,800 RPM

GEARS: 6

DRY WEIGHT: 215 KG

MAX SPEED: 299 KM/H (186 MPH)

FUEL TANK CAPACITY: 18 LITRES

COLOURS: BLUE & BLACK, BLUE & SILVER, SILVER

COST: £8,299

Triumph Daytona 955i

The Triumph Daytona 955i is a sport bike manufactured by Triumph from 1997 to 2006. It was powered by a 955 cc liquid-cooled, 3-cylinder, 4-stroke engine. The bike was launched in 1997 as the Triumph T595 Daytona and renamed Triumph Daytona 955i in 1999.

The Triumph was powerful, but also heavy. It weighed 20 kg more than the Honda Fireblade (see p.11).

DID YOU KNOW?

A Daytona was featured in *Mission Impossible 2*, which starred Tom Cruise.

This is the Triumph Speed-Twin. It was first made in 1937 and continued to be made for over 20 years.

The Daytona had a 'naked' brother called the Speed Triple. It had the same engine and chassis, but no fairing.

STATS & FACTS

LAUNCHED: 1997

ORIGIN: UK

ENGINE: 955 CC

CYLINDERS: 3

MAXIMUM POWER: 147 BHP AT 10,700 RPM

MAXIMUM TORQUE: 100 NM AT 8,200 RPM

GEARS: 6

DRY WEIGHT: 191 KG

MAXIMUM SPEED: 265.5 KM/H (165 MPH)

FUEL TANK CAPACITY: 21 LITRES

COLOURS: JET BLACK, ACIDIC YELLOW, TORNADO RED

COST: £8,799

Originally a maker of musical instruments, Yamaha started making motorcycles after World War II. In 2009, Yamaha produced a new version of its open-class sport bike, the YZF-R1. The engine technology came from the M1 Moto GP bike driven by Valentino Rossi, with its cross-plane crankshaft and irregular firing intervals.

DID YOU KNOW?

A new throttle control allows the rider to choose between three distinct modes, depending on the rider's environment.

A subframe in magnesium cast in a carbon fibre mould makes the bike both strong and light.

The front features dual projector headlights integrated with the air induction intakes. This accentuates the aerodynamic look of the YZF R1 and gives it an aggressive supersport image.

STATS & FACTS

LAUNCHED: 2009

ORIGIN: JAPAN

ENGINE: 998 CC

CYLINDERS: 4

MAXIMUM POWER: 179BHP AT 12,500 RPM

MAXIMUM TORQUE: 115.5 NM AT 10,000 RPM

GEARS: 6

DRY WEIGHT: 206 KG

MAXIMUM SPEED: 293 KM/H (182 MPH)

FUEL TANK CAPACITY: 18 LITRES

COLOURS: CADMIUM YELLOW, RAVEN/CANDY RED, PEARL WHITE/ RAPID RED, TEAM YAMAHA BLUE/ WHITE

COST: £13,399

ACCELERATION Making a bike go faster by opening the throttle.

AERODYNAMIC A shape that cuts through the air around it.

AIR INTAKES Large scoops that direct air into the engine, sucking in extra fuel to give a bike more power.

ALUMINIUM A lightweight, strong metal.

BHP Brake horse power, the usual measure of an engine's power.

BODYWORK PLASTIC panels that cover the chassis and engine.

BRAKES Part of a bike used to slow it down.

CARBON FIBRE A very light, but strong, material.

CC Cubic capacity, the measurement used for the size of the engine.

CHASSIS See *Frame*.

CYLINDER The part of the engine where fuel is burned to make energy.

ENGINE The part of the bike where the fuel is burned to create energy.

EXHAUST PIPE at the back of the bike where poisonous gases made when gasoline is burned are let out. The exhaust is also used to reduce engine noise.

FAIRING Part of the bike covering the engine whose function is to produce a smooth outline so the motorcyle goes faster.

FANS Part of the bike that pushes or pulls cool air through the radiator, helping to cool the engine.

FORKS Fork-shaped tubes that secure the front wheel and handlebars.

FRAME The part of the bike that holds the engine, wheels and bodywork together. Also called the chassis.

GEARS System that lets a bike change speed without harming the engine.

HEADLIGHT The bright light at the front of the bike.

LED Light Emitting Diode, a source of light used in some brake lights.

LINKED BRAKES System where the front brake lever also works the back brake, and the back brake lever works the front brake.

PERIMETER BRAKES Braking system where the brake disc is mounted around the edge of the wheel.

RADIAL BRAKES Braking system where the brake discs are mounted at the bottom of the forks, parallel to the wheel.

RADIATOR Part of the bike that uses water to stop the engine from overheating.

RPM Revolutions (revs) of the engine per minute.

SPORTS BIKE A fast motorcycle that has been developed for road use.

SUPERBIKE A fast motorcycle that is very similar to a racing motorcycle.

SUSPENSION Springs and shock absorbers attached to a motorcycle's wheels, giving a smooth ride in spite of bumps in the road.

TANK Hollow metal unit where petrol is stored.

THROTTLE The part of a bike that is used to make it go faster or slower.

TORQUE AND NM The measurements for an engine's power.

TURBO System that increases a bike's power by forcing more air into the engine.

TYRE A rubber covering for a wheel, filled with compressed air.

Index

A

aerodynamics 23, 29
Agusta
  see MV Agusta
aluminium 20
Aprilia 4, 5
  RSV Mille R 4, 5
Audi 20

B

Benelli, Tornado 6, 7
Benelli Mechanical
  Workshop 6
Benelli, Teresa 6
Blackbird 10, 11, 25
Boselli, Earls 14
brakes 12
  linked 10
  perimeter 9
  radial 5, 15
British Land Speed
  Record 24
Buell, XB9R Firebolt 8
Buell, Erik 8

C

Cagiva 18, 19
  V-Raptor 1000 18, 19
carbon fibre 15, 20, 28
Castiglioni,
  Giovanni 18
chassis 27
Cruise, Tom 26
cylinders 19

D

Daytona 26, 27
drive belt 8
Ducati 20, 21
  1199 21
  999 series 20, 21

E

emblems 17, 21
engines 6, 12
  Harley 8
  Hayabusa 24
  Porsche 16
exhausts 8

F

fairing 15, 27, 30
fans 7
Fireblade 11, 26
Firebolt 8, 9
footrests 19, 20
frames 6, 28

G

Galluzzi, Miguel 18
Grand Prix 22

H

Harley, V-Rod 16, 17
Harley-Davidson 8,
  16, 17
Hayabusa 10, 24, 25
headlights 5,
  12, 22, 29
Hell's Angels 16
Honda 10, 11, 15, 24, 26
  CBR900RR
    Fireblade 11, 26
  CBR1100XX
    Blackbird 10, 11, 25

K

Kawasaki 12, 13
  Ninja ZX-12R 12,
  Ninja ZX-14R 13
Knievel, Evel 16

L

lights 29
linked braking 10

M

Mille R 4, 5
Mission Impossible
  (film) 26
Mondial 14, 15
  Piega 14, 15
mopeds 4
Morton, Adrian 6
MV Agusta 22, 23
  F4 SPR Senna 22, 23

N

"naked" sportbikes
  18, 27
Ninja ZX-12R 12,
Ninja ZX 14-R 13

P

Piega 14, 15
Porsche 16

R

radiators 7
Rosa, Riccardo 7

S

seats 7, 17, 20
Senna, Ayrton 22
single seaters 4
speed 4, 10, 11, 12
Speed Triple 27
Speed-Twin 27
suspension 6
Suzuki 10, 24, 25
  GSX 1300R Hayabusa
    10, 24, 25
  Hayabusa 2011 25

T

Tornado 6, 7
Triumph 26, 27
  Daytona 955i 26, 27
  Daytona Speed
    Triple 27
  Speed-Twin 27
turbo-charge 24
two seaters 4

V

V-Raptor 1000
  18, 19
V-Rod 16, 17
Varese 18

W

World Superbike
  series 7

Y

Yamaha 28, 29
  YZF R1 28, 29